Mel, the Red Blood Cell

Smile Little Earth

Dedicated to my cousins

who have given me
unconditional love and support.

Hey there,

My name is Mel.

I live in your blood

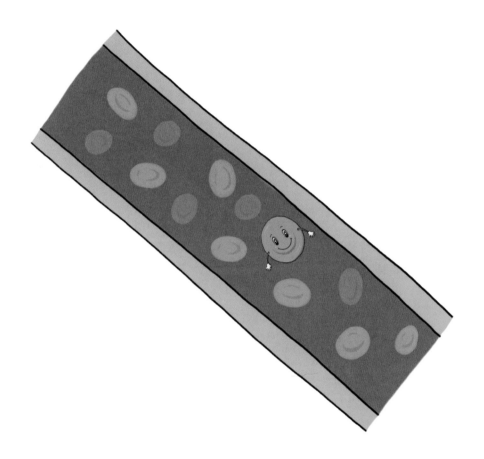

Because I'm a red blood cell.

I carry oxygen, carbon dioxide,

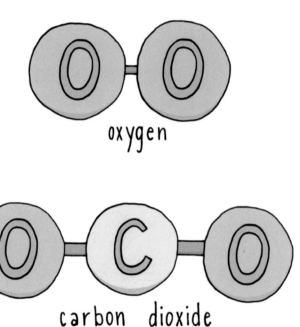

oxygen

carbon dioxide

And other molecules.

I deliver them in your body

So my job is pretty cool.

Let's go to where my job begins

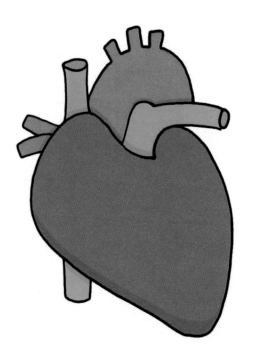

Inside the heart.

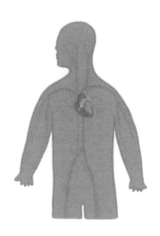

The right and left atrium and ventricle

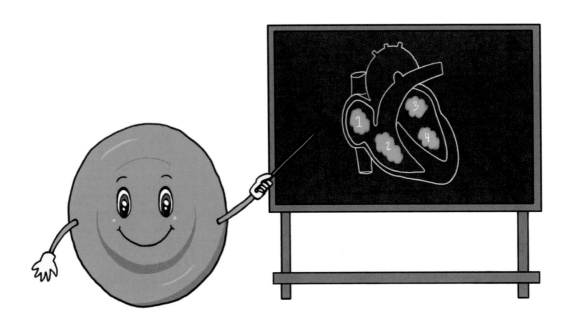

Are some of its parts.

I start out with carbon dioxide
and no oxygen,

That's why I'm blue.

So I go into the right atrium

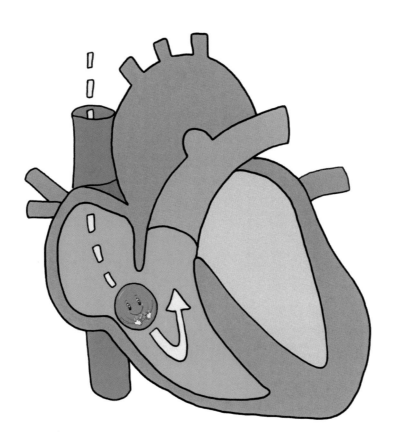

And the right ventricle too.

Next into the pulmonary artery

And then to the lungs I turn.

Where I give away my carbon dioxide

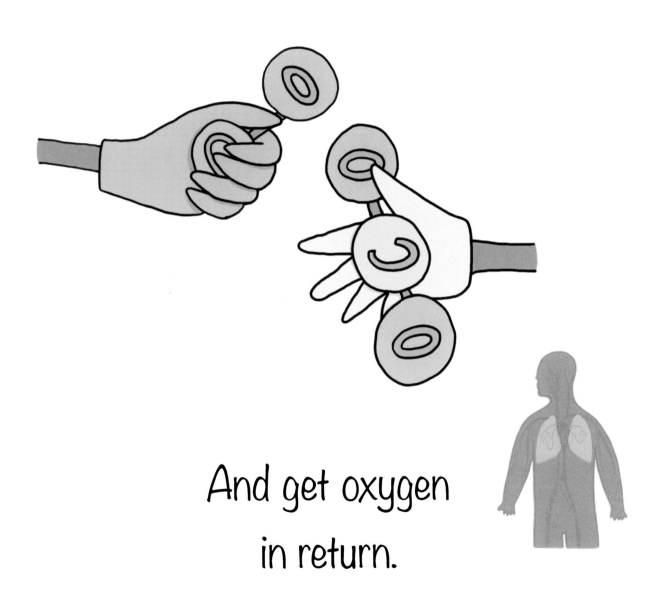

And get oxygen
in return.

Now that I'm red,

Since I have oxygen with me,

I go back to the heart

So I can deliver it to your body.

I enter the left atrium

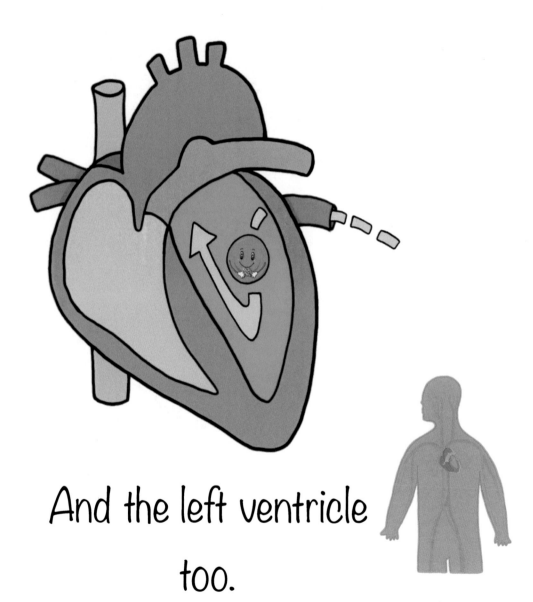

And the left ventricle
too.

Next the aorta

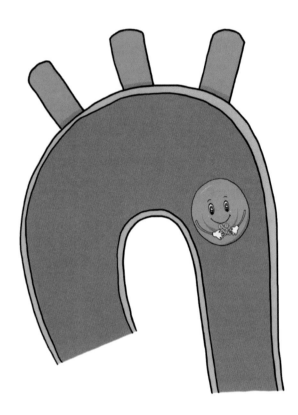

Is what I go through.

With my oxygen in hand

I go on a journey.

Going through lots of tunnels

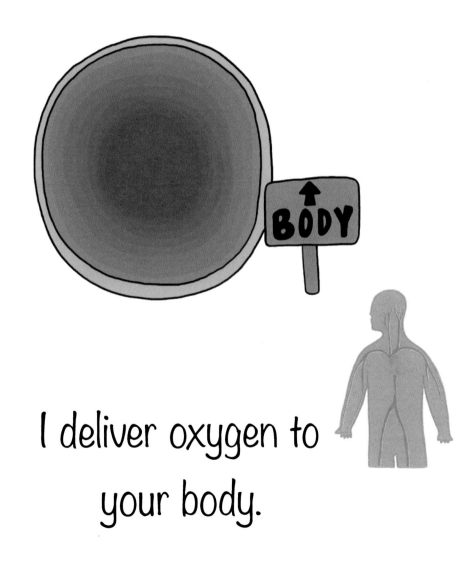

I deliver oxygen to your body.

My job is important since

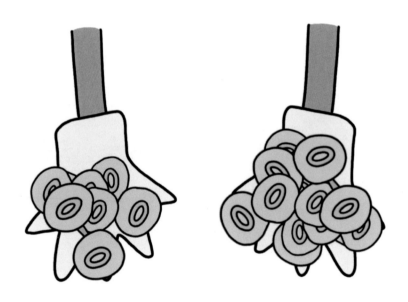

The oxygen I carry

Helps you walk, run, climb, and jump

Because it gives you energy.

In return I get carbon dioxide

And then I go back
to the heart.

Once I enter it again

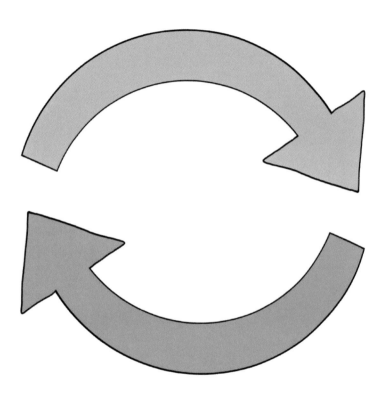

The process restarts.

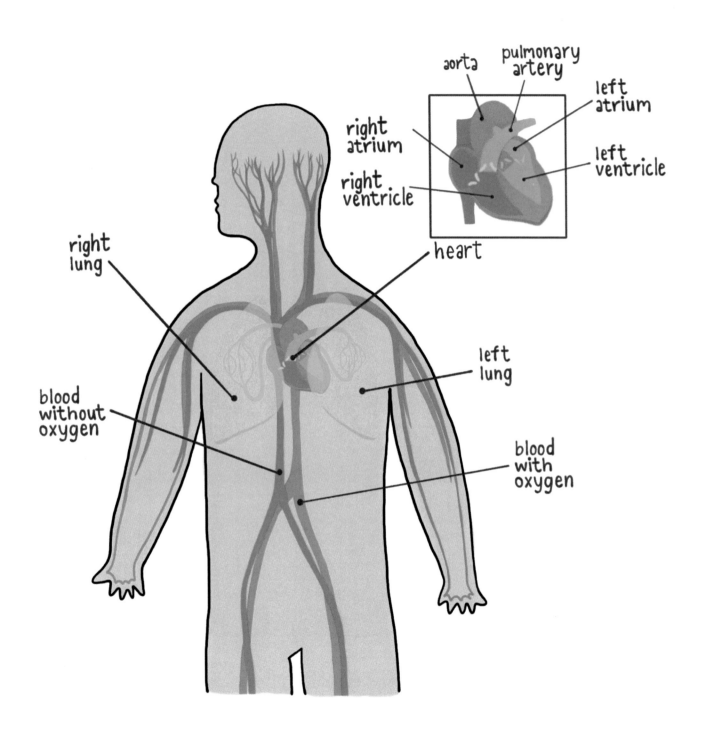

aorta

pulmonary artery

right atrium

left atrium

right ventricle

left ventricle

heart

right lung

left lung

blood without oxygen

blood with oxygen

About the Author

I am a high school student who enjoys playing squash, dancing, singing, and traveling. I live with my family and my dog in California. I love writing, drawing, and making videos especially for kids. My last few books were "Oops! I'm Early", "Bye Bye, Cookie", and "Yippee! I'm Home."

More books in this series:
"Uh Oh! Gotta Go"

Made in the USA
Las Vegas, NV
23 July 2021